THE AMAZING COSMIC COLORING BOOK

Illustrated by Joan C. Gratz

ISBN 10 1535220279
ISBN 13   9781535220279

Illustrated by Joan C. Gratz

Colored by

Illustrated by Joan C. Gratz

Colored by

Illustrated by Joan C. Gratz

Colored by

Illustrated by Joan C. Gratz

Colored by

Illustrated by Joan C. Gratz

Colored by

Illustrated by Joan C. Gratz

Colored by

Illustrated by Joan C. Gratz

Colored by

Illustrated by Joan C. Gratz

Colored by

Illustrated by Joan C. Gratz

Colored by

Illustrated by Joan C. Gratz

Colored by

Illustrated by Joan C. Gratz

Colored by

Illustrated by Joan C. Gratz

Colored by

Illustrated by Joan C. Gratz

Colored by

Illustrated by Joan C. Gratz

Colored by

Illustrated by Joan C. Gratz

Colored by

Illustrated by Joan C. Gratz

Colored by

Illustrated by Joan C. Gratz

Colored by

Illustrated by Joan C. Gratz

Colored by

Illustrated by Joan C. Gratz

Colored by

Illustrated by Joan C. Gratz

Colored by

Illustrated by Joan C. Gratz

Colored by

Illustrated by Joan C. Gratz

Colored by

Illustrated by Joan C. Gratz

Colored by

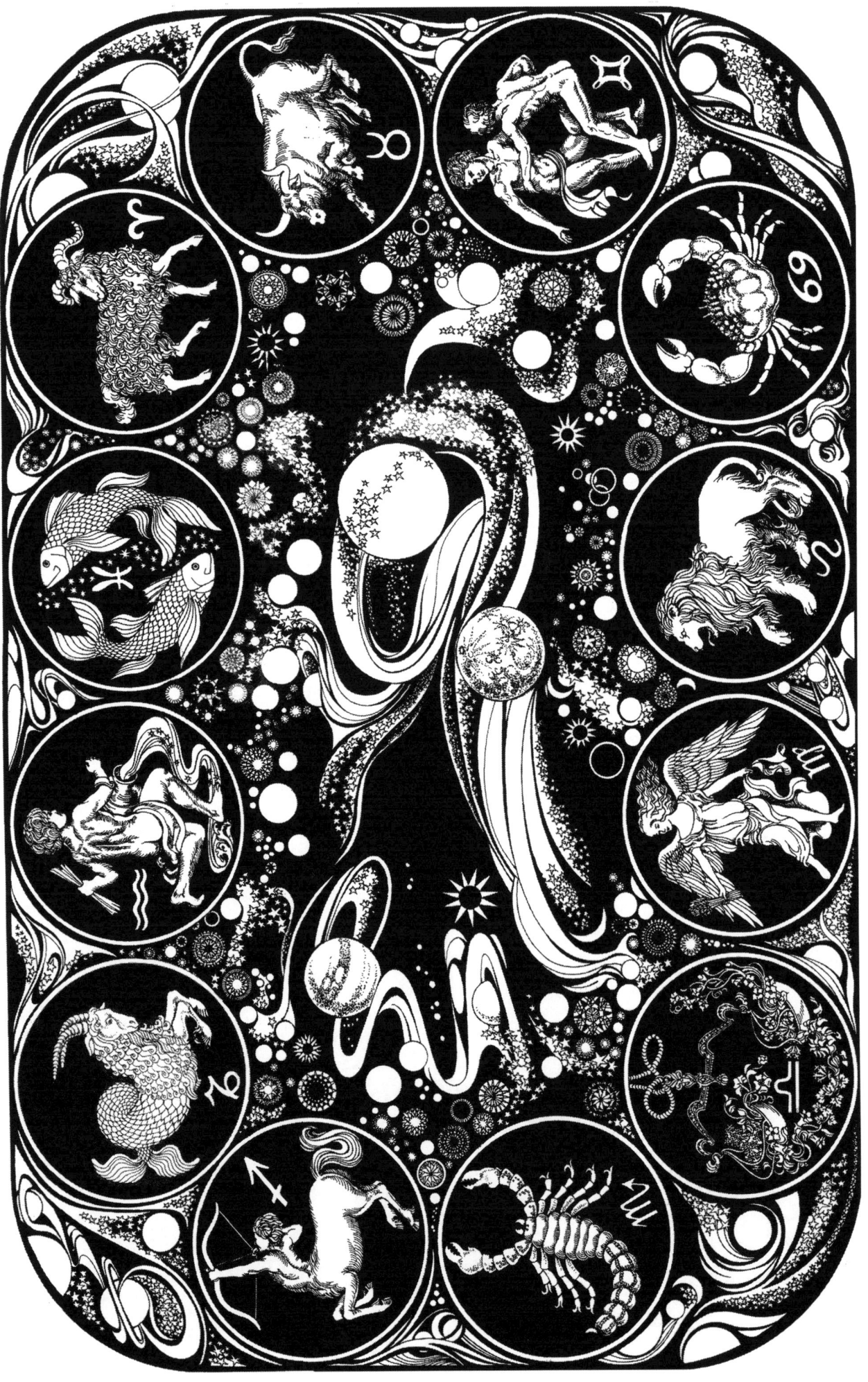

Illustrated by Joan C. Gratz

Colored by

Illustrated by Joan C. Gratz

Colored by

Illustrated by Joan C. Gratz

Colored by

Illustrated by Joan C. Gratz

Colored by

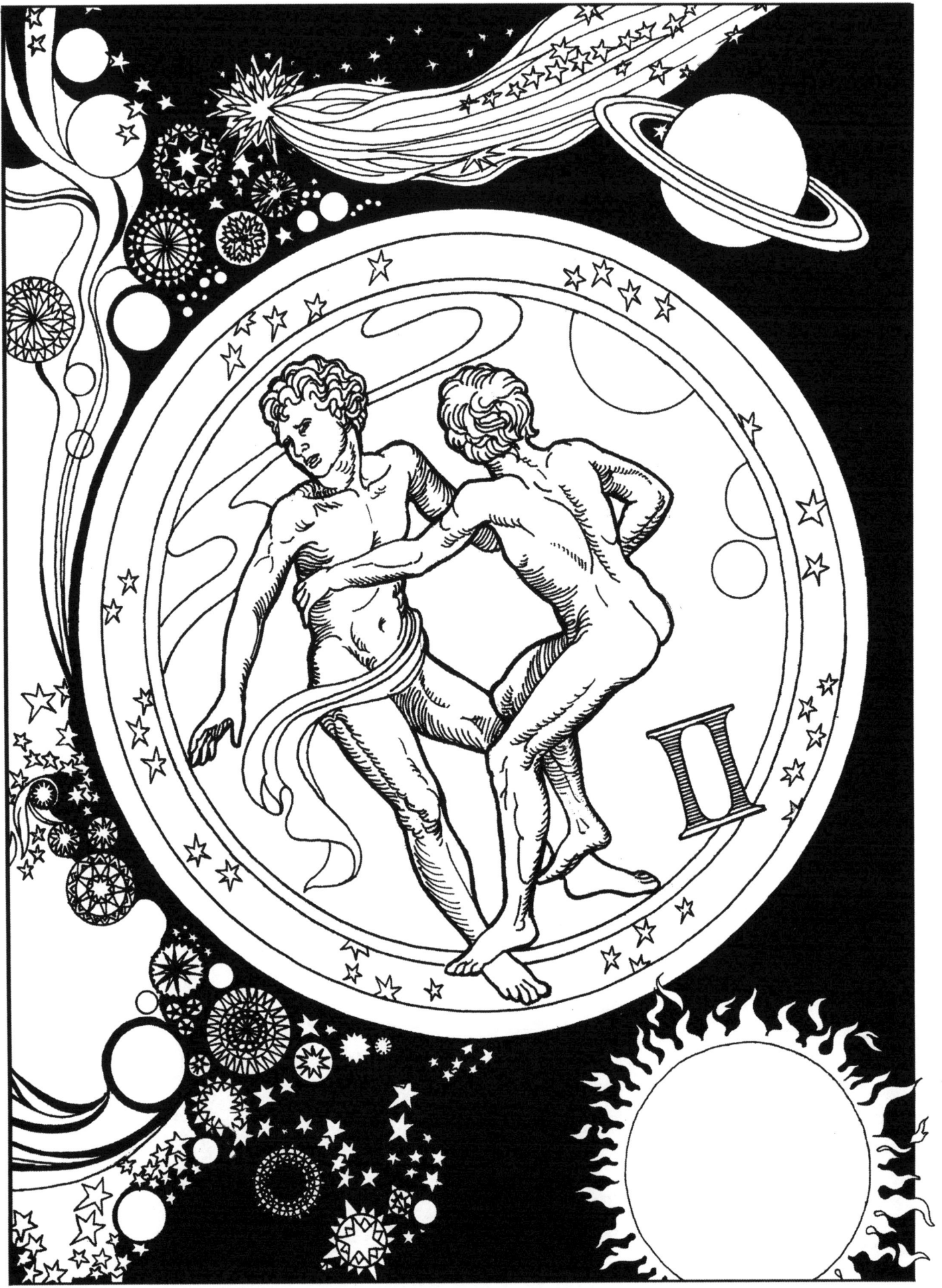

Illustrated by Joan C. Gratz

Colored by

Illustrated by Joan C. Gratz

Colored by

Made in the USA
Middletown, DE
24 December 2016